Practical Applications of Category Theory in Computer Science

Written By Richard Aragon

Introduction

In the ever-evolving landscape of computer science, the quest for powerful abstractions that simplify complex problems and foster deeper understanding is an ongoing endeavor. Category theory, once considered an esoteric branch of mathematics, has emerged as a surprising and potent ally in this pursuit.

This book, "Practical Applications of Category Theory in Computer Science," aims to bridge the gap between the theoretical foundations of category theory and its concrete applications in various domains of computer science. We will embark on a journey that begins with the fundamental concepts of categories, objects, morphisms, functors, and natural transformations. These building blocks, often cloaked in mathematical abstraction, will be demystified and illuminated through relatable examples and practical use cases.

Why Category Theory for Computer Science?

Category theory provides a unique lens through which to view and analyze complex systems. Its emphasis on relationships, structure, and composition resonates deeply with the challenges faced by computer scientists. Whether you're grappling with the intricacies of software architecture, striving for elegance in functional programming, or seeking innovative solutions in machine learning, category theory offers a fresh perspective and a powerful toolkit.

Target Audience and Prerequisites

This book is designed for intermediate to advanced programmers and computer scientists who are curious about the theoretical underpinnings of their craft and eager to explore new tools for tackling complex problems. While some familiarity with programming concepts and mathematical notation is assumed, we will strive to make the material accessible to readers from diverse backgrounds.

What to Expect

In the pages that follow, we will:

- **Unravel the Core Concepts:** We'll explore the fundamental ideas of category theory, providing intuitive explanations and illustrative examples drawn from the world of computer science.
- **Dive into Applications:** We'll delve into the practical applications of category theory in various domains, including functional programming, software architecture, data modeling, machine learning, quantum computing, distributed systems, formal verification, and programming language design.
- **Bridge Theory and Practice:** We'll demonstrate how abstract categorical concepts translate into concrete solutions for real-world problems, empowering you to apply category theory in your own work.

A Journey of Discovery

This book is not just a technical manual; it's an invitation to embark on a journey of discovery. As you explore the elegant and powerful world of category theory, you'll gain new insights into the nature of computation, the structure of data, and the design of software systems. You'll discover a language that allows you to express complex ideas with clarity and precision, and a framework that guides you towards more elegant and robust solutions. So, let's dive in and explore the practical applications of category theory in computer science!

Chapter 1: Category Theory Unveiled – A Programmer's Perspective

1.1 Why Should Programmers Care About Category Theory?

Category theory, often dubbed "abstract nonsense" for its high level of abstraction, might seem far removed from the daily grind of coding. But beneath this reputation lies a powerful toolset with surprising practicality. It's a language for describing structures and transformations, offering a fresh lens through which we can view and solve complex problems in computer science.

If you've ever grappled with:

- **Managing complexity in large software systems:** Category theory offers principles for modular design and compositionality.
- **Understanding the essence of data types and their relationships:** Category theory provides a framework for thinking about types and their operations.
- **Designing flexible and reusable code:** Category theory's emphasis on abstraction can lead to elegant and adaptable solutions.

...then you might find category theory to be a valuable ally. It won't magically solve every problem, but it equips you with a new way of thinking, often leading to more elegant and insightful solutions.

1.2 A Gentle Introduction to the Language of Categories

At its core, category theory deals with:

- **Objects:** Think of these as the nouns in our language. They represent the things we're interested in – data types, programs, or even whole systems.
- **Morphisms (or arrows):** These are the verbs, describing relationships or transformations between objects. A morphism might be a function converting one data type to another, or a program transforming an input to an output.

These basic building blocks combine to form **categories**. A category is simply a collection of objects and morphisms, governed by a few simple rules:

1. **Composition:** Morphisms can be chained together. If you have a morphism f from object A to B, and another morphism g from B to C, you can compose them to get a new morphism $g \circ f$ (read "g after f") that goes directly from A to C.
2. **Identity:** Every object has an identity morphism, which acts like the number 1 in multiplication – it doesn't change anything.

That's it! These two simple rules, along with a few additional concepts we'll explore, open up a vast landscape of possibilities.

1.3 An Appetizer: Functors and Natural Transformations

While objects and morphisms form the foundation, category theory offers a rich vocabulary for expressing more sophisticated ideas. Let's briefly sample two essential concepts:

- **Functors:** These are mappings between categories. They preserve the structure of the source category, translating its objects and morphisms into corresponding elements in the target category. Think of them as translators between different languages, ensuring that the meaning of sentences is preserved in the translation.
- **Natural Transformations:** These describe relationships between functors. They tell us how two different translations are related, ensuring that they're consistent with each other in a specific way.

We'll delve into these concepts more deeply later on, but this glimpse should give you a taste of the expressive power of category theory.

1.4 What's Next?

In the following chapters, we'll explore how these abstract ideas translate into concrete tools for programmers. We'll see how category theory can guide us in designing software architectures, understanding type systems, and even tackling challenges in machine learning. Buckle up – the journey into the world of category theory is about to get exciting!

Chapter 2: Categories and Types – A Match Made in Abstraction Heaven

2.1 From Sets to Categories: A Shift in Perspective

Most programmers have a solid grasp of set theory. We use sets to represent collections of data, and functions to transform data from one set to another. Category theory takes this familiar foundation and elevates it to a new level of abstraction.

Instead of focusing on the elements within sets, category theory shifts our attention to the relationships between sets. Remember, a category consists of objects (which could be sets) and morphisms (which could be functions). This shift in focus allows us to reason about the structure of data and transformations in a more abstract and flexible way.

2.2 Types as Objects, Functions as Morphisms

In the world of programming, **types** are essentially sets with some additional structure. They define the possible values a variable can hold and the operations that can be performed on those values. In a categorical setting, we can naturally view types as objects and functions between types as morphisms.

Let's consider a simple example:

```
int add(int x, int y) {
    return x + y;
}
```

The function add takes two integers as input and produces an integer as output. In categorical terms, we'd say add is a morphism from the object Int × Int (the product of the integer type with itself) to the object Int.

2.3 Composition and Identity: The Rules of the Game

Remember the two fundamental rules of categories:

1. **Composition:** We can compose the add function with itself to create a new function that adds three integers:

```
int add3(int x, int y, int z) {
    return add(add(x, y), z);
}
```

In category theory, we'd say that the morphism add3 is the composition of add with itself.

2. **Identity:** Every type has an identity function that simply returns its input unchanged:

```
int identity(int x) {
    return x;
}
```

This seemingly trivial function plays a crucial role in category theory, ensuring that every object has a "do-nothing" morphism associated with it.

2.4 Beyond Functions: Polymorphism and Generics

Category theory can handle more sophisticated concepts like polymorphism and generics. For example, a generic function like:

```
T identity<T>(T x) {
    return x;
}
```

can be viewed as a family of morphisms, one for each type T. This idea extends to more complex generic structures like containers and algorithms.

2.5 What's the Point?

By viewing types and functions through the lens of category theory, we gain several benefits:

- **Abstraction:** We can reason about the behavior of functions without getting bogged down in the details of specific data types.
- **Compositionality:** We can build complex functions by composing simpler ones, leading to more modular and maintainable code.
- **Generality:** We can develop generic algorithms and data structures that work across a wide range of types.

2.6 Onward to More Advanced Structures

In the next chapters, we'll explore more advanced categorical structures like functors, natural transformations, and monads. These concepts might seem abstract, but they have surprisingly practical applications in areas like functional programming, data modeling, and software architecture. Get ready to see how category theory can transform the way you think about code!

Chapter 3: Functors – Translating Structure Across Categories

3.1 Functors: The Mappings of Categories

In the previous chapter, we saw how categories can model individual collections of types and functions. But what if we want to express relationships between different categories? This is where functors come in.

A **functor** is a mapping between categories that preserves their structure. It takes objects from one category and maps them to objects in another category, and it also takes morphisms and maps them to morphisms, all while respecting the rules of composition and identity. Think of a functor as a translator between different languages, ensuring that the meaning of sentences is preserved in the translation.

3.2 Functors in Programming: Examples and Applications

Functors are pervasive in programming, even if you haven't called them by that name. Here are a few examples:

- **List Functor:** In many programming languages, the `List` type constructor is a functor. It takes a type `T` and produces the type `List<T>`. It also takes a function `f: T -> U` and maps it to a function `map(f): List<T> -> List<U>`, which applies `f` to each element of the list.
- **Option Functor:** The `Option` type (also known as `Maybe`) represents the possibility of absence of a value. It is a functor because it can map functions over the potential values it contains.
- **Mapping Over Data Structures:** Functors provide a unified way to apply functions to elements within various data structures, such as trees, graphs, and dictionaries.

3.3 Functors and Composition: The Harmony of Structure

The true power of functors lies in their ability to compose. If we have two functors, `F: C -> D` and `G: D -> E`, we can compose them to get a new functor `G ∘ F: C -> E`. This means we can chain together transformations across multiple categories, ensuring that the structure is preserved at each step.

3.4 Functors and Type Constructors: A Deeper Connection

Many type constructors in programming languages are naturally functors. For example, consider a simple binary tree type constructor:

data Tree a = Leaf a | Node (Tree a) (Tree a)

We can define a functor instance for Tree:

```
instance Functor Tree where
    fmap f (Leaf x) = Leaf (f x)
    fmap f (Node l r) = Node (fmap f l) (fmap f r)
```

This allows us to apply functions to the values stored in the tree, regardless of its shape.

3.5 Why Functors Matter

Functors are a powerful abstraction that allows us to:

- **Generalize operations:** We can define operations that work on a wide range of data types by abstracting over functors.
- **Preserve structure:** We can transform data within complex structures without losing their essential relationships.
- **Compose transformations:** We can build complex transformations by combining simpler ones in a modular way.

3.6 Onwards to Natural Transformations

In the next chapter, we'll explore another key concept in category theory: natural transformations. These provide a way to relate different functors, adding another layer of abstraction and expressiveness to our toolbox. Prepare to see how functors and natural transformations work together to form a powerful framework for reasoning about structure and transformation in computer science.

Chapter 4: Natural Transformations – Morphisms Between Functors

4.1 Beyond Functors: Relationships Between Transformations

Functors provide a way to map between categories, preserving structure. But what if we want to express relationships between *different functors*? This is where natural transformations step in.

A **natural transformation** is a way of transforming one functor into another functor while respecting the structure of the categories involved. It's like a family of morphisms, each one connecting a specific object in one functor's image to the corresponding object in another functor's image.

4.2 Visualizing Natural Transformations

Imagine two functors, F and G, both mapping from category C to category D. A natural transformation α from F to G can be visualized as a collection of arrows, one for each object in C:

```
F(A) ---α_A---> G(A)
 |         |
F(f)      G(f)
 |         |
F(B) ---α_B---> G(B)
```

Each arrow $α\_A$ is a morphism in category D, connecting the object $F(A)$ to the object $G(A)$. The "naturality" condition ensures that these arrows are compatible with the morphisms in C. In other words, if we have a morphism $f: A \rightarrow B$ in C, then the following diagram must commute:

```
F(A) ---α_A---> G(A)
 |         |
F(f)      G(f)
 |         |
F(B) ---α_B---> G(B)
```

4.3 Natural Transformations in Programming

Natural transformations show up in various corners of programming:

- **Converting Between Data Representations:** Consider functors representing different data structures (e.g., lists and trees). A natural transformation can provide a way to convert between these representations while preserving the underlying data.
- **Adapting Interfaces:** In object-oriented programming, natural transformations can be used to adapt objects to different interfaces, allowing them to be used in various contexts.
- **Generalizing Algorithms:** By abstracting over natural transformations, we can write algorithms that work with a wide range of data structures and interfaces.

4.4 The Power of Naturality

The naturality condition might seem like a technical detail, but it has profound consequences. It ensures that natural transformations are structure-preserving, meaning they respect the relationships between objects and morphisms in the categories involved. This makes them a powerful tool for reasoning about transformations and equivalences between functors.

4.5 Onwards to Higher-Order Structures

With functors and natural transformations under our belt, we're ready to tackle even more advanced concepts in category theory. In the following chapters, we'll explore higher-order structures like monads, which provide a way to model computations with effects. Get ready to see how category theory can unlock new levels of abstraction and expressiveness in your code!

Chapter 5: Monads – Composing Computations with Effects

5.1 Beyond Pure Functions: The World of Effects

So far, we've mostly focused on pure functions, which take inputs and produce outputs without any side effects. However, most real-world programs interact with the outside world, performing actions like reading from files, writing to databases, or making network requests. These actions introduce side effects that can make reasoning about code more challenging.

Category theory provides a powerful tool for managing effects in a principled way: monads.

5.2 Monads: The Containers of Computations

A **monad** is a structure that represents a computation with potential side effects. It's like a container that wraps a value, along with the necessary machinery to sequence and combine computations in a controlled manner.

A monad consists of:

- **A type constructor** `M`: This defines the type of computations that the monad represents. For example, the `Maybe` monad represents computations that might fail, while the `IO` monad represents computations that interact with the external world.
- **A `return` function:** This takes a value of type `a` and wraps it in the monad `M a`. It represents a pure computation that simply returns a value.
- **A `bind` (or `>>=`) operator:** This takes a computation `M a` and a function `a -> M b`, and it produces a new computation `M b`. It allows us to chain computations together, passing the result of one computation as input to the next.

5.3 Monads in Action: Examples and Applications

Monads are ubiquitous in functional programming:

- **Error Handling (Maybe/Option):** The `Maybe` monad provides a clean way to handle errors by propagating failure through a sequence of computations.
- **Input/Output (IO):** The `IO` monad captures all interactions with the external world, ensuring that side effects are explicitly represented and controlled.
- **State Management (State):** The `State` monad allows us to model computations that depend on and modify some underlying state.

5.4 The Monad Laws: The Contract of Composition

To ensure that monads behave in a predictable way, they must satisfy three laws:

1. **Left identity:** `return a >>= f` is equivalent to `f a`
2. **Right identity:** `m >>= return` is equivalent to `m`
3. **Associativity:** `(m >>= f) >>= g` is equivalent to `m >>= (\x -> f x >>= g)`

These laws guarantee that monadic computations compose correctly, regardless of the specific monad being used.

5.5 Why Monads Matter

Monads might seem like a theoretical curiosity, but they provide several benefits:

- **Explicit effects:** They make side effects explicit, leading to more predictable and easier-to-reason-about code.
- **Compositionality:** They allow us to compose complex computations with effects in a modular way.
- **Abstraction:** They abstract over different types of effects, leading to more generic and reusable code.

5.6 Monads and Category Theory

Monads have a deep connection to category theory. In fact, they are a specific kind of monoid in the category of endofunctors. This connection provides a rich theoretical foundation for understanding and working with monads.

5.7 Onwards to Practical Applications

In the following chapters, we'll delve into practical applications of category theory in various areas of computer science, including functional programming, software architecture, and even machine learning. Get ready to see how these abstract ideas can lead to concrete improvements in your code!

Chapter 6: Category Theory in Action – Functional Programming Unleashed

6.1 Functional Programming: A Natural Fit for Category Theory

Functional programming (FP) emphasizes pure functions, immutable data, and higher-order functions. This focus aligns beautifully with the concepts we've explored in category theory.

- **Categories as Function Composition:** FP heavily relies on composing functions to build larger programs. Category theory provides a rigorous framework for understanding this composition, ensuring that functions can be chained together reliably.
- **Functors as Higher-Order Functions:** Many higher-order functions in FP, such as `map`, `filter`, and `fold`, are essentially functors. They lift functions to operate on different data structures, preserving the structure of those structures.
- **Monads for Effects:** FP languages often use monads to manage effects like input/output, state, and exceptions. This provides a principled way to handle side effects while maintaining the purity of core functions.

6.2 Category Theory in Haskell: A Showcase of Abstraction

Haskell, a purely functional language, embraces category theory as a core design principle. Let's see how some of the concepts we've covered translate into Haskell code:

- **Types as Objects, Functions as Morphisms:** Haskell's type system directly mirrors the categorical notions of objects and morphisms. Types like `Int`, `Bool`, and `Maybe a` are objects, and functions like `(+): Int -> Int -> Int` and `not: Bool -> Bool` are morphisms.
- **Functors in Action:** Haskell's `Functor` typeclass captures the essence of functors. It requires a type to implement the `fmap` function, which lifts a function over the type's values. For example, the list type `[]` is a functor, and `fmap` applies a function to each element of a list.
- **Monads for Effects:** Haskell uses monads extensively to handle effects. The `IO` monad captures all interactions with the outside world, the `Maybe` monad handles potential failure, and the `State` monad manages mutable state.

6.3 Beyond Haskell: Category Theory in Other FP Languages

Category theory isn't limited to Haskell. Many other functional programming languages, such as Scala, F#, and OCaml, have also adopted categorical concepts. Even non-functional languages like Python and JavaScript can benefit from the insights of category theory.

6.4 Category Theory: A Guiding Principle for Software Design

Beyond its direct application in functional programming, category theory provides a valuable perspective for software design in general. The emphasis on abstraction, compositionality, and structure preservation can lead to more flexible, reusable, and maintainable code.

For example, designing software components as functors can make them easier to compose and adapt to different contexts. Using monads to manage effects can lead to more predictable and easier-to-reason-about code.

6.5 Onwards to New Frontiers

Category theory is a vast and evolving field with many exciting applications yet to be discovered. As we continue to explore its depths, we're likely to uncover new ways to apply these powerful concepts to solve complex problems in computer science. The journey into the world of category theory is just beginning!

Chapter 7: Category Theory and Software Architecture – Blueprints for Modularity and Composition

7.1 From Monolithic to Modular: The Challenge of Complexity

As software systems grow in complexity, managing that complexity becomes a critical challenge. Monolithic architectures, where all components are tightly coupled, often become unwieldy and difficult to maintain. This is where modular design comes in.

Modular design involves breaking down a system into smaller, self-contained components that interact through well-defined interfaces. This approach promotes reusability, maintainability, and scalability.

7.2 Category Theory as a Blueprint for Modularity

Category theory provides a powerful framework for thinking about modularity. The concepts of objects, morphisms, functors, and natural transformations can be used to model components, their interactions, and their transformations.

- **Components as Objects:** Each component in a system can be represented as an object in a category. The object encapsulates the component's internal state and behavior, while its interface is represented by the morphisms it can participate in.
- **Interactions as Morphisms:** The interactions between components can be modeled as morphisms. A morphism from component A to component B represents a function call or a message passing from A to B.
- **Functors for Adaptation:** Functors can be used to adapt components to different contexts. For example, a functor can transform a component that operates on one data type into a component that operates on another data type.
- **Natural Transformations for Compatibility:** Natural transformations ensure that different functors are compatible with each other. For example, a natural transformation can ensure that two different functors that operate on lists and trees can be used interchangeably.

7.3 Designing with Categories: A Modular Approach

By applying these concepts, we can design software systems in a more modular and composable way:

1. **Identify Components:** Start by identifying the key components of your system. Each component should have a clear responsibility and a well-defined interface.
2. **Model Interactions:** Define the interactions between components as morphisms. This will help you understand the dependencies between components and how they work together.

3. **Use Functors for Adaptation:** If you need to adapt a component to a different context, use a functor to transform it. This will allow you to reuse components in different parts of your system.
4. **Ensure Compatibility with Natural Transformations:** If you have multiple functors, use natural transformations to ensure they are compatible with each other. This will make your system more flexible and adaptable.

7.4 Category Theory in Practice: Examples and Tools

Category theory has already influenced the design of several software systems and frameworks:

- **Functional Reactive Programming (FRP):** FRP frameworks like Elm and ReactiveX use category theory to model reactive systems, where changes in one component can trigger changes in other components.
- **Scalable Component Architectures:** Frameworks like Scala's Cats and Haskell's Arrows provide tools for building scalable component architectures based on category theory.
- **Microservices:** The principles of modularity and composition, which are central to category theory, are also essential for designing microservices architectures.

7.5 Beyond Modularity: Category Theory and System Properties

Category theory can also help us reason about system-level properties like correctness, security, and performance. By modeling system components and their interactions as categories, we can use categorical tools to prove theorems about the behavior of the system.

7.6 Conclusion

Category theory provides a powerful framework for thinking about software architecture. By applying its concepts, we can design systems that are more modular, composable, reusable, and maintainable. The journey into the world of category theory is not just a theoretical exploration, but a practical guide to building better software.

Chapter 8: Category Theory and Data Modeling – Relationships, Structure, and Abstraction

8.1 Beyond Entities and Relationships: A New Perspective on Data

Traditional data modeling often focuses on entities (the things we store data about) and relationships (the connections between entities). While this approach is useful, it can sometimes feel limiting when dealing with complex data structures and transformations.

Category theory offers a fresh perspective on data modeling, emphasizing relationships and transformations rather than just individual entities. This shift in focus allows us to model complex data structures in a more natural and flexible way.

8.2 Categories as Data Models: Objects, Morphisms, and Beyond

In a categorical data model, we can represent entities as objects and relationships as morphisms. For example, in a social network, users might be objects, and friendships between users might be morphisms.

But category theory goes beyond simple entities and relationships. It allows us to model more complex structures like:

- **Hierarchies:** We can represent hierarchical relationships (e.g., parent-child relationships in a tree structure) using categories with special morphisms that denote inclusion or inheritance.
- **Graphs:** We can model graphs, where nodes represent entities and edges represent relationships, using categories where morphisms can have multiple sources and targets.
- **Data Transformations:** We can model data transformations (e.g., converting raw data into a structured format) using functors that map between different categories.

8.3 Schema Evolution and Category Theory

Schema evolution, the process of modifying a database schema over time, can be a challenging task. Category theory can help us approach this problem in a more structured way.

By representing database schemas as categories, we can use functors and natural transformations to model schema transformations. For example, a functor might represent a migration script that transforms one schema into another, while a natural transformation might ensure that the data in the old schema can be mapped to the new schema.

8.4 Category Theory in Practice: Data Modeling Tools

Category theory has already influenced the design of several data modeling tools:

- **GraphQL:** The GraphQL query language uses the concept of a schema, which can be seen as a category of types and fields.
- **Category Theory for Databases (CTDB):** This research project explores the use of category theory for designing and querying databases.
- **Datomic:** This database uses a data model based on entities, attributes, and values, which can be represented as a category.

8.5 Beyond Data Modeling: Category Theory and Data Analysis

Category theory is not just useful for modeling data; it can also help us analyze and reason about data. For example, we can use category theory to define concepts like similarity and distance between data points, and to design algorithms for clustering and classification.

8.6 Conclusion

Category theory provides a powerful and flexible framework for data modeling. By shifting our focus from entities to relationships, we can model complex data structures in a more natural way. And by using functors and natural transformations, we can model schema evolution and data transformations in a more structured way. The journey into the world of category theory is not just a theoretical exploration, but a practical guide to understanding and working with data.

Chapter 9: Category Theory and Machine Learning – A Match Made in Abstraction?

9.1 Machine Learning: A Playground for Structure and Transformation

At its core, machine learning (ML) is about finding patterns in data and using those patterns to make predictions or decisions. This involves representing data in various ways, transforming it through algorithms, and composing those algorithms to create complex models.

Sound familiar? These activities align closely with the concepts we've explored in category theory.

9.2 Categories and Neural Networks: A Natural Connection

One of the most promising areas of overlap is between category theory and neural networks. Neural networks are essentially complex compositions of transformations, and category theory provides a natural language for describing these compositions.

- **Layers as Morphisms:** Each layer in a neural network can be viewed as a morphism, transforming data from one representation to another.
- **Composition of Layers:** The composition of layers in a neural network can be modeled as the composition of morphisms in a category.
- **Neural Architectures as Categories:** Entire neural architectures can be seen as categories, where objects represent different layers or types of data, and morphisms represent the transformations betweenthem.

9.3 Functors and Transformations in Machine Learning

Functors also play a role in machine learning. For instance, the process of feature engineering, where we transform raw data into a format suitable for a model, can be viewed as a functor that maps one category (raw data) to another (features).

Additionally, natural transformations can be used to relate different feature representations or model architectures.

9.4 Monads for Probabilistic Modeling

Many machine learning algorithms involve probabilistic modeling, where we reason about uncertain quantities. Monads, with their ability to represent computations with effects, provide a natural way to model probabilistic computations. For example, the probability monad can represent distributions over values, and monadic operations can be used to combine and transform distributions.

9.5 Category Theory in Practice: ML Frameworks and Tools

While the application of category theory to machine learning is still an active area of research, there are already some tools and frameworks that leverage these concepts:

- **Catlab:** This Julia library provides a framework for building composable and differentiable models using category theory.
- **DisCoPy:** This Python library uses category theory to model distributed systems and computations.
- **Categorical Probabilistic Programming (CPP):** This research area explores the use of category theory for probabilistic programming.

9.6 Challenges and Opportunities

Applying category theory to machine learning is not without its challenges. One challenge is the high level of abstraction, which can make it difficult to translate theoretical concepts into practical implementations. Another challenge is the need for more research to fully understand the connections between category theory and machine learning.

However, the potential benefits are significant. Category theory could provide a more rigorous foundation for machine learning, leading to better algorithms, models, and tools. It could also help us bridge the gap between theory and practice, making machine learning more accessible to a wider audience.

9.7 Conclusion

The relationship between category theory and machine learning is still in its early stages, but it holds immense promise. By applying the principles of category theory, we can gain deeper insights into the structure of data, the transformations we apply to it, and the models we build. This could lead to a new generation of machine learning tools and techniques that are more powerful, flexible, and easy to use.

Chapter 10: Category Theory and Quantum Computing – A Dance of Abstraction and Quantum Weirdness

10.1 Quantum Computing: A New Paradigm of Computation

Quantum computing is a revolutionary paradigm that leverages the principles of quantum mechanics to perform computations that are impossible for classical computers. It has the potential to transform fields like cryptography, drug discovery, and materials science.

At its core, quantum computing deals with quantum systems, which can exist in superpositions of states and exhibit entanglement. These quantum phenomena are inherently different from the classical world, and they require new mathematical tools to describe and manipulate them.

10.2 Category Theory as a Language for Quantum Mechanics

Category theory, with its focus on abstraction, compositionality, and structure preservation, turns out to be a surprisingly well-suited language for describing quantum systems and their transformations.

- **Quantum Systems as Objects:** Quantum systems, such as qubits or quantum circuits, can be represented as objects in a category. The object encapsulates the system's state space and the possible operations that can be performed on it.
- **Quantum Processes as Morphisms:** Quantum processes, such as measurements or quantum gates, can be represented as morphisms between quantum systems. The morphism describes how the state of a system evolves under the action of a process.
- **Composition of Processes:** The composition of quantum processes can be modeled as the composition of morphisms in a category. This allows us to reason about the sequential application of quantum gates and measurements.

10.3 ZX-Calculus: A Categorical Approach to Quantum Circuits

One of the most exciting applications of category theory in quantum computing is the ZX-calculus. This graphical calculus provides a way to represent quantum circuits as diagrams, where nodes represent quantum gates and wires represent qubits. The ZX-calculus is based on category theory, and it provides a powerful framework for reasoning about quantum circuits, optimizing them, and even discovering new quantum algorithms.

10.4 Beyond ZX-Calculus: Category Theory in Quantum Foundations

Category theory is not just a tool for manipulating quantum circuits. It also has the potential to shed light on the foundational questions of quantum mechanics. For example, researchers are exploring how category theory can help us understand the nature of quantum entanglement, the measurement problem, and the emergence of classical physics from the quantum world.

10.5 Challenges and Opportunities

The application of category theory to quantum computing is still a young field, but it is rapidly growing. There are many challenges to overcome, such as developing efficient algorithms for simulating quantum systems and designing new quantum programming languages that can leverage the power of category theory.

However, the potential rewards are immense. Category theory could provide a new foundation for quantum computing, leading to breakthroughs in algorithm design, error correction, and fault-tolerant quantum computation. It could also help us understand the fundamental nature of quantum mechanics, opening up new avenues for scientific discovery.

10.6 Conclusion

The intersection of category theory and quantum computing is a fascinating frontier of research. By applying the abstract tools of category theory, we can gain deeper insights into the complex world of quantum mechanics and unlock the full potential of quantum computing. The journey into this quantum realm is just beginning, and it promises to be an exciting adventure.

Chapter 11: Category Theory and Distributed Systems – Taming Complexity through Abstraction

11.1 Distributed Systems: A Web of Interactions

Distributed systems, consisting of multiple interconnected components that communicate and collaborate, are the backbone of modern computing. They power everything from cloud platforms to social networks to financial systems. However, their inherent complexity poses significant challenges in terms of design, implementation, and verification.

11.2 Category Theory as a Compass in the Distributed Landscape

Category theory, with its focus on structure, composition, and abstraction, offers a valuable framework for navigating the intricacies of distributed systems. It provides tools for modeling complex interactions, reasoning about system behavior, and even verifying correctness properties.

- **Components as Objects:** Each component in a distributed system (e.g., servers, clients, databases) can be represented as an object in a category. The object encapsulates the component's state and behavior, while its interface is defined by the morphisms it can participate in.
- **Communication as Morphisms:** The communication channels between components, such as network connections or message queues, can be modeled as morphisms. A morphism from component A to component B represents a message sent from A to B.
- **Protocols as Functors:** Communication protocols, which define the rules for how components interact, can be modeled as functors. A functor transforms messages from one format to another, ensuring compatibility between different components.
- **System Behavior as Compositions:** The overall behavior of a distributed system can be understood as the composition of morphisms. This allows us to reason about the flow of information and the dependencies between components.

11.3 Category Theory in Action: Examples and Applications

Category theory has already found applications in various aspects of distributed systems:

- **Actor Model:** The actor model, a popular framework for concurrent and distributed systems, has strong connections to category theory. Actors can be seen as objects, messages as morphisms, and actor systems as categories.
- **Process Calculi:** Process calculi, formal languages for describing concurrent systems, have been given categorical interpretations. This allows us to apply categorical tools to reason about the behavior of concurrent processes.
- **Distributed Data Structures:** Category theory can be used to model and reason about distributed data structures, such as distributed hash tables and blockchains.

11.4 Towards a Categorical Foundation for Distributed Computing

Researchers are actively exploring the use of category theory to provide a more solid foundation for distributed computing. This includes:

- **Developing Categorical Models:** Creating categorical models that capture the essential properties of distributed systems, such as concurrency, communication, and fault tolerance.
- **Designing Categorical Programming Languages:** Designing programming languages that are specifically tailored for distributed systems, leveraging the concepts of category theory.
- **Verifying Distributed Systems:** Using categorical tools to verify the correctness of distributed systems, ensuring that they behave as intended even in the presence of failures.

11.5 Challenges and Opportunities

Applying category theory to distributed systems is not without its challenges. The complexity of these systems can make it difficult to find suitable abstractions. Additionally, the dynamic nature of distributed systems, where components can come and go, requires models that can handle change.

However, the potential rewards are significant. Category theory could provide a more rigorous foundation for distributed computing, leading to better design principles, more reliable systems, and more powerful tools for verification and analysis.

11.6 Conclusion

Category theory offers a fresh perspective on distributed systems, allowing us to tackle their complexity with the power of abstraction. By modeling components, communication, and protocols using categorical concepts, we can gain deeper insights into the behavior of these systems and build more reliable, scalable, and efficient solutions. The journey into the categorical world of distributed computing is just beginning, and it holds immense promise for the future of software development.

Chapter 12: Category Theory and Formal Verification – Proving Correctness with Mathematical Rigor

12.1 Formal Verification: Ensuring Software Reliability

Software bugs can have catastrophic consequences, from financial losses to safety hazards. Formal verification is a rigorous approach to ensuring software correctness by using mathematical proofs to guarantee that a program behaves as intended.

Traditional testing can only uncover the presence of errors, not their absence. Formal verification, on the other hand, can provide strong guarantees about the absence of errors under certain assumptions.

12.2 Category Theory as a Foundation for Formal Verification

Category theory, with its emphasis on abstraction and formal reasoning, provides a natural foundation for formal verification. The concepts of categories, functors, and natural transformations can be used to model program behavior, specify correctness properties, and construct proofs.

- **Programs as Morphisms:** In a categorical setting, programs can be viewed as morphisms between data types. This allows us to reason about the transformation of data as it flows through a program.
- **Specifications as Categories:** Correctness properties can be specified as categories, where objects represent program states and morphisms represent valid transitions between states.
- **Proofs as Functors:** A proof that a program satisfies a specification can be represented as a functor that maps the program's behavior category to the specification category.

12.3 Category Theory in Practice: Verification Tools and Techniques

Category theory has already influenced the design of several formal verification tools and techniques:

- **Coq:** This proof assistant uses a type theory that is closely related to category theory. It allows users to write programs and specifications in a formal language and then construct proofs that the programs satisfy the specifications.
- **Isabelle/HOL:** This proof assistant also uses a type theory with strong connections to category theory. It has been used to verify a wide range of software systems, including operating systems, compilers, and cryptographic protocols.
- **Category Theory for Program Verification:** This research area explores the use of category theory for developing new verification techniques, such as model checking and abstract interpretation.

12.4 Beyond Code Verification: Category Theory and System Design

Category theory can also be used to guide the design of software systems that are easier to verify. By applying categorical principles like compositionality and abstraction, we can create systems that are more modular, easier to reason about, and more amenable to formal verification.

12.5 Challenges and Opportunities

Applying category theory to formal verification is not without its challenges. One challenge is the need for expertise in both category theory and formal methods. Another challenge is the scalability of verification techniques, as verifying complex systems can be computationally expensive.

However, the potential rewards are significant. Category theory could provide a more powerful and expressive framework for formal verification, leading to stronger correctness guarantees and more reliable software. It could also help us bridge the gap between theory and practice, making formal verification more accessible to software developers.

12.6 Conclusion

Category theory is a powerful tool for formal verification, allowing us to reason about the correctness of software systems with mathematical rigor. By applying categorical concepts, we can model program behavior, specify correctness properties, and construct proofs. The journey into the categorical world of formal verification is just beginning, and it holds immense promise for the future of software reliability.

Chapter 13: Category Theory and Programming Language Design – Types, Semantics, and Beyond

13.1 Programming Languages: A Universe of Abstractions

Programming languages are tools of immense power, enabling us to express complex ideas and instruct machines to perform intricate tasks. They provide abstractions that allow us to manipulate data, control flow, and manage resources. Category theory, with its focus on abstraction and structure, offers a unique perspective on the design and analysis of programming languages.

13.2 Categories as the Backbone of Type Systems

Type systems play a crucial role in programming languages, ensuring that operations are performed on compatible data types and preventing errors. Category theory provides a solid foundation for type systems, allowing us to express complex type relationships and derive type inference rules.

- **Types as Objects:** In a categorical type system, types are represented as objects in a category. This allows us to model complex type relationships, such as subtyping, polymorphism, and generics, using categorical concepts.
- **Type Constructors as Functors:** Type constructors, which allow us to create new types from existing ones (e.g., lists, pairs, functions), can be modeled as functors. This enables us to reason about how type transformations affect the underlying data.
- **Type Inference as Composition:** Type inference, the process of automatically determining the types of expressions, can be viewed as a composition of morphisms in a category. This provides a formal basis for type inference algorithms.

13.3 Semantics and Category Theory: Meaningful Programs

Semantics is the study of the meaning of programs. Category theory provides a powerful framework for expressing program semantics, allowing us to reason about the behavior of programs in a precise and abstract way.

- **Denotational Semantics:** This approach interprets programs as mathematical objects, such as functions or relations. Category theory provides a natural way to express these interpretations, using categories to model domains of values and morphisms to model program functions.
- **Operational Semantics:** This approach defines program behavior in terms of state transitions. Category theory can be used to model state spaces and transition systems, providing a rigorous foundation for operational semantics.

13.4 Category Theory in Practice: Programming Language Design

Category theory has already influenced the design of several programming languages:

- **Haskell:** This purely functional language is heavily influenced by category theory. Its type system, module system, and many of its libraries are based on categorical concepts.
- **ML-family Languages:** Languages like OCaml and F# have also adopted categorical ideas, particularly in their type systems and module systems.
- **Dependently Typed Languages:** These languages, like Agda and Idris, use category theory to express complex type dependencies and proofs of correctness.

13.5 Beyond Type Systems and Semantics: Category Theory in Language Features

Category theory is not just relevant to the foundations of programming languages. It can also be used to design and analyze specific language features, such as:

- **Concurrency and Parallelism:** Category theory can be used to model concurrent and parallel computations, ensuring that they are free from race conditions and deadlocks.
- **Effect Systems:** These systems, which track and manage side effects, can be modeled using categorical concepts like monads and arrows.
- **Metaprogramming:** Category theory can provide a framework for designing metaprogramming features, which allow programs to manipulate other programs.

13.6 Conclusion

Category theory is a powerful tool for programming language designers. By applying its concepts, we can create languages that are more expressive, type-safe, and reliable. The journey into the categorical world of programming languages is just beginning, and it holds immense promise for the future of software development.

Glossary and Key Terms

Category: A collection of objects and morphisms, along with rules for composing morphisms and an identity morphism for each object. Categories serve as a framework for describing relationships and transformations between entities in a structured way.

Object: An entity within a category, representing a concept, data type, or system. Objects are the nouns in the language of category theory.

Morphism (or Arrow): A connection or transformation between objects in a category. Morphisms can represent functions, processes, or any relationship that respects the structure of the category.

Composition: The act of combining two morphisms to create a new one. In a category, morphisms can be composed if the target object of the first morphism matches the source object of the second morphism.

Identity Morphism: A special morphism for each object that acts like the number 1 in multiplication; it doesn't change the object when composed with another morphism.

Functor: A mapping between categories that preserves the structure of the source category. It maps objects to objects and morphisms to morphisms, respecting composition and identities. Functors act as translators between categories.

Natural Transformation: A way to transform one functor into another functor while respecting the structure of the categories involved. It can be visualized as a family of morphisms, each one connecting objects in one functor's image to the corresponding objects in another functor's image.

Monad: A structure that represents a computation with potential side effects. Monads consist of a type constructor, a `return` function, and a `bind` (or `>>=`) operator, and they adhere to specific laws that guarantee the correct composition of monadic computations.

Monoid: A set equipped with an associative binary operation and an identity element. Monoids are a fundamental algebraic structure with connections to category theory.

Adjunction: A relationship between two categories, where each category has a functor to the other, and these functors are related in a specific way. Adjunctions play a crucial role in category theory, expressing deep connections between different mathematical structures.

Limit and Colimit: Ways of constructing new objects in a category from existing ones. Limits and colimits generalize familiar concepts like products, coproducts, and equalizers, and they provide a powerful tool for describing relationships between objects.

Yoneda Lemma: A fundamental theorem in category theory that states that an object in a category is completely determined by the morphisms going into it or out of it. The Yoneda lemma has far-reaching implications, connecting seemingly different areas of mathematics and computer science.

Category Theory: The study of abstract structures and relationships between them, using the language of categories, functors, and natural transformations. Category theory has applications in various fields, including mathematics, computer science, physics, and philosophy.

By understanding these key terms, you'll be well-equipped to explore the fascinating world of category theory and its diverse applications in computer science.

References

1. **Barr, M., & Wells, C. (2012). Category Theory for Computing Science (3rd ed.).** This is a comprehensive and widely used textbook on category theory, tailored specifically for computer scientists. It covers the fundamentals of category theory and delves into its applications in various areas of computer science.
2. **Pierce, B. C. (2002). Types and Programming Languages.** While not exclusively focused on category theory, this book provides a thorough introduction to type systems and their foundations, often using categorical concepts to explain type relationships and transformations.
3. **Awodey, S. (2010). Category Theory (2nd ed.).** This book offers a more mathematically oriented introduction to category theory, delving into its foundations and connections to other areas of mathematics.
4. **Spivak, D. I. (2014). Category Theory for the Sciences.** This book takes a unique approach, applying category theory to various scientific disciplines, including physics, biology, and economics. It demonstrates the versatility of category theory as a tool for modeling and reasoning about complex systems.
5. **Milewski, B. (2019). Category Theory for Programmers.** This online book provides a hands-on introduction to category theory, using code examples in Haskell to illustrate concepts. It's a great resource for programmers who want to learn category theory in a practical context.